Original title:
Walls That Whisper

Copyright © 2025 Creative Arts Management OÜ
All rights reserved.

Author: Eleanor Prescott
ISBN HARDBACK: 978-1-80587-022-7
ISBN PAPERBACK: 978-1-80587-492-8

The Heartbeat Behind Closed Doors

Behind the door, the laughter sings,
A cat debates the joys of flings.
The kettle's dance, a comical sight,
As socks engage in playful fights.

The clock ticks loud, as if to tease,
While shadows play with matchstick knees.
A dance of dust, a playful truce,
As echoes giggle at the moose.

Unspoken Histories Lurking Near

In every crack, a story hides,
A sneaky tale of silly rides.
The brass doorknob twinkles bright,
As sneezes make the echoes fight.

The hallway bends with secret glee,
Whispering jokes to the old oak tree.
A rubber chicken's fate is sealed,
In raucous laughter, past revealed.

The Silence of Unseen Divides

Between the walls, where secrets flow,
A mouse in pants steals center show.
The silence cracks with comic grace,
As furniture joins the funny race.

The ceiling whispers snickers low,
While memories burst like popcorn, whoa!
An invisible hug, a gentle pat,
A giggle lingers with the cat.

Memories Trapped in Mortar

Embedded laughs in bricks confined,
A comical past, so well aligned.
Each flake of paint, a chuckling ghost,
Of awkward dances, we treasure most.

In dusty corners, laughter stays,
As echoes bounce in quirky ways.
A rubber band once flung too far,
Still giggles soft beneath the bar.

Echoes of Secrets

In the corner, a tale untold,
Chairs giggle where dust grew old.
Teapots chuckle, secrets they brew,
Whispers of mischief, just between you.

Pictures grin, with eyes so sly,
As if they've seen each pie in the sky.
The cat on the shelf gives a wink,
Who knows more than we could think?

Shadows Between the Stones

In the garden, a gnome takes a stand,
Confess your sins to a plastic band.
Rabbits gossip under leafy crowns,
While daisies spread the juiciest sounds.

Beneath the bricks, two mice share a joke,
About the broom that refused to poke.
A toad starts a rumor, froggy delight,
As fireflies dance in the soft moonlight.

Murmurs of the Enclosed

In the attic, an old trunk creaks,
Full of laughter, it sneaks and squeaks.
A pair of socks in a tussle, you see,
Debating if they should fly free.

A clock chuckles, each tick a surprise,
Peeking at us with clever eyes.
The broom and bucket start to jest,
Competing for who is the best.

Memories Encased in Silence

In the corner, the couch tells a joke,
Recounting the time the cat was awoke.
Vases roll their eyes at old creaky tales,
While curtains snicker at length of the scales.

A pencil grins, hidden under a book,
Sharing stories with paper, what a look!
The carpet hums a tune quite sweet,
As shoes tap dance to the whimsical beat.

The Embrace of Timeless Grit

In a city where laughter bounces,
Old bricks gossip and share their pounces.
They watch the joggers with fits of grace,
While hiding crumbs of a long-lost race.

Pigeons strut like they own the shop,
With a flair that makes all the humans stop.
They squawk their opinions and let them fly,
As the sun paints shadows that wave goodbye.

Graffiti smiles like a jester's face,
Telling tales of this wild place.
The echoes chuckle, the laughter ensues,
While the concrete sighs with colorful hues.

So next time you stroll past a stoic stone,
Remember it's more than just a big bone.
It's a comic performance, a playful stage,
Where even the quiet can be all the rage.

A Tapestry Woven in Stone and Shadow

In the alleyways where shadows prance,
Old bricks harmonize in a cheeky dance.
They weave their stories through cracks and lines,
Laughing at time while sipping on wines.

A dog in a hat gives a sassy bark,
While the lampposts nod like they own the park.
Each pebble chuckles at all the fuss,
As the cats roll their eyes in a fluffy bus.

The murals grinning with colors bold,
Share secrets of love and dreams untold.
While pigeons crack jokes at the passersby,
Underneath the laughter, the moments fly.

So tip your hat to this quirky place,
Join in the fun, don't lose your grace.
For in every crevice, there's a giggle that grows,
A tapestry made of life's little shows.

Ephemeral Tunes of Urban Secrets

Listen close to the echoes that play,
They sprinkle giggles in a breezy ballet.
Graffiti sings while the traffic hums,
As cheeky whispers dance with the drums.

The sidewalk cracks hold secrets profound,
Like a treasure chest where humor is found.
Sneaky cats plotting their delightful schemes,
While strolls turn into whimsical dreams.

A bicycle horn beeps a playful tune,
As squirrels debate the best way to swoon.
They scamper around with mischievous flair,
While twinkling stars barely notice, they're there.

So roam through the city, let joy be your guide,
Embrace the laughter that waits at your side.
In this maze of whispers, hilarity rings,
As urban mysteries and laughter takes wings.

Interludes in the Hushed Landscape

A peek behind the door, oh dear,
Where socks parade and chairs play near.
A secret world of dust and cheer,
Where even roaches quip, no fear.

The fridge hums jokes, a sassy tune,
As leftovers join the waltz 'til noon.
Spices gossip while pans swoon,
Together they craft a funny rune.

The broom does tango, a messy play,
Cans and jars join in the fray.
Each corner smiles, what do they say?
"Who knew the floor could dance this way?"

In silence, laughter hides its glee,
While cobwebs wave like flags, you see.
The shadowy cat nods knowingly,
In this hushed place, joy's the decree.

Eulogy of the Overlooked Abode

Here lies a house of pastel dreams,
With windows cracked and faded beams.
The dust accumulates, or so it seems,
While squirrels plot, oh how it teems.

In corners, grumpy gnomes now rust,
They roll their eyes with heaps of dust.
The stairs complain, it's a must,
A creaky tune, in them we trust.

Chairs mob together, gossip flows,
About that cat with too many toes.
Pesky pigeons charade their shows,
While curtains bear the tales that grows.

Yet here, the laughter's often heard,
Amongst the echoes, each strange word.
An ode to things, not all perturbed,
In this abode, quirks are preferred.

Silence Woven into the Fabric of Structures

A tapestry of quiet, oh so wide,
Holds stories where giggles hide.
The creaky ceiling beams provide,
A backdrop where silliness resides.

Cushions whisper, secrets shared,
As mischievous raccoons declared:
"The kitchen's a mess but we're not scared,
For snacks await, it's fully aired."

The wooden floorboards crack a joke,
While a timid mouse dons a cloak.
In stillness, laughter softly broke,
The say-so of a sleepy bloke.

With each soft sigh of the sun,
These silly tales can't be outrun.
Structures laugh, just a little fun,
In this absurd world, we're all one.

Muffled Laments in Cinder Trails

Amidst the bricks, the giggles bloom,
In shadows cast, they start to loom.
A brick sneezed, oh what a doom,
Yet laughter's breath dispels the gloom.

The garden gnome, a sassy chap,
Wore a cap that looked like a map.
He tripped on roots, fell in a lap,
In tickled chaos, all minds snap.

Pigeons prattle, gossip that flies,
While squirrels plan their pranks and lies.
With every flutter, joy multiplies,
In this quirk-filled space, nothing dies.

So tread with care on ground that sings,
For here, the silence is pulled by strings.
Unearth the chuckles, the joy it brings—
In muffled murmurs, laughter springs.

Specters in the Grotto

In a cave where echoes play,
The ghosts compile their grand buffet.
With snacks they've found from days of yore,
They dance and twirl 'til hearts implore.

A phantom chef with pots ablaze,
Serves soup that smells of yesterdays.
Yet every sip's a funny prank,
As brown and green, it surely stank.

They tell tall tales of ancient lore,
While hiding behind the balmy door.
With each loud laugh, stones start to quake,
And bats, like shuttles, join the wake.

So if you hear a giggling shout,
In darkened caves, don't fear, don't pout.
For specters here just want to play,
And brighten up your gloomy day.

The Resonance of Enclosure

Inside a box where secrets dwell,
A toad plays tunes, oh what a swell!
With frogs as backup, croaking clear,
They serenade the mice who cheer.

Each thump and bump makes creatures laugh,
As they attempt a daring half.
But critters slip and tumble back,
In chases round the squeaky track.

Listen close, hear giggles rise,
As moles in tuxes dance and prize.
Their tiny feet in perfect time,
With jumpy beats—oh what a prime!

So when you're stuck, just look around,
In silly places fun can be found.
With every thrum and rattle loud,
Let joyous notes grow like a cloud!

Secrets Immured in Silence

A closet hides a talking sock,
With tales of adventures, around the clock.
It dreams of fame on the runway bright,
But trips on laces, what a sight!

In corners where old secrets twine,
The whispers of paperclips align.
They giggle about the paper's plan,
To dress a frog, a real-life fan!

With silence thick, a tickled sneeze,
Turns dull gray walls into a tease.
For laughter echoes through the mute,
Like a punny pun of a mustache flute.

So open doors to where they hide,
Find strange delights that won't be denied.
In every nook, don't stand in fright,
Just join the fun, and laugh till night!

Phrases Etched in the Shadows

In dim-lit corners, jokes reside,
With whispers playing hide and slide.
Old riddles stuck like chewing gum,
Set to crack each time we hum.

The shadows weave hilarious tales,
Of ships that sailed with wobbly sails.
They poke at suns that lost their glow,
And dancing clouds that put on shows.

Each phrase etched plays a funny trick,
As snickering tries to sneak a flick.
For in the dark, we find such cheer,
With shadows that bring the jokes quite near.

So hear them laugh, those shapes that play,
In angled beams where giggles sway.
Join the whispers, let loose the glee,
For life's too short to bend your knee!

In the Embrace of Echoing Bricks

Old bricks giggle in the sun,
Hiding secrets, oh what fun!
They share jokes with the passing breeze,
While squirrels crack up in the trees.

A pigeon coos a silly rhyme,
Infecting pigeons, oh so prime.
The paint peels off with a grin,
Laughing at all the stories within.

Underneath the arching stone,
Whispers of laughter softly blown.
A ghost who lost his sense of fate,
Now hosts parties, isn't that great?

Chimneys chuckle, how absurd,
Carrying tales, they're quite the nerds.
Echoing glee in every nook,
Take a peek and read the book!

Soft Voices of the Frozen Past

The windows shiver, tales galore,
As icebergs chime and softly snore.
Laughter trapped in crystal freeze,
Tickling toes with a gentle breeze.

A chair squeaks with a silly cheer,
It cracks a joke, and we all hear.
Memories giggle in the frost,
Playing hide and seek — who's lost?

The clock chuckles, it's running late,
Holding songs from a distant date.
Footsteps fumble on the floor,
Old slippers dance forevermore.

Whispers waltz through every crack,
Chasing ghosts on a merry track.
In this frost, we all take part,
It's comedy straight from the heart!

Chords of the Unseen

Strings of laughter hang in air,
Plucking hearts with a silly flair.
Jokes flutter by like fragile notes,
Drifting dreams in rainbow coats.

Ghostly giggles, they intertwine,
With whispers of a punchline fine.
Every eavesdrop, a riotous feat,
Chords of laughter, scatter and meet.

Beneath the surface, they play a tune,
Causing grins under the moon.
Shadows shimmy, in rhythmic delight,
Dancing echoes, oh what a sight!

Silly melodies float through the air,
As unseen friends join the affair.
Each strum brings chuckles, sweet as pie,
Tickling ribs as the stars sigh!

The Soliloquy of Structures

In crumbling corners, wise ones chat,
Surveying life with a well-worn pat.
Every beam holds a playful jest,
Offering laughs, they know best.

Post and lintel whisper out loud,
Making friends with every crowd.
Columns flap like pocket wings,
Share their quips with jovial rings.

Rooftops chime with muffled glee,
In the breeze, a giggling spree.
Every crack a punchline made,
In this comedy parade.

Echoes dance on wooden beams,
Hosting parties of crazy dreams.
Structures sigh and snicker too,
For each moment is something new!

Phantoms Lurking in Soft Shadows

In the corner, shadows peek,
With little giggles, they cheekily sneak.
A phantom in a top hat, oh what a sight,
Doing the cha-cha on the stairs at night.

The cat gives a jump, then a curious glare,
As they dance in the moonlight without a care.
Who knew ghosts had such rhythm and flair?
I think I'll join and try not to scare.

Musings on the Edge of Perception

Round the bend, I ponder and muse,
What's hidden in the thoughts I choose?
A thought bubble pops, like a balloon,
It's full of giggles and a tune!

A mirror grins with a wink and a smile,
Reflecting my thoughts in a cheeky style.
What if the world were made of cheese?
I'd slice and serve it, if you please!

Faint Echoes in the Twilight Air

In twilight's glow, a giggle floats,
From shadows that wear mismatched coats.
Do they have secrets, or just a bad joke?
A rascal in disguise, or a friendly bloke?

They whisper sweet nothings, oh so sly,
Like cartoons plotting to make me cry.
"Why did the ghost cross the road?" they tease,
"To haunt the other side, if you please!"

Whispers Held by Timeless Structures

In a creaky house that dreams and sighs,
A chatter of whispers fills the skies.
A door swings wide with a squeaky grin,
"Who wants to join in? Let the fun begin!"

Timeless walls with stories to share,
A riddle or two? Please, pull up a chair!
They've seen the chaos of laughter and tears,
And hold all the giggles of countless years.

Veins of Time in Urban Landscapes

In the city streets where pigeons trot,
Stories hide in every parking spot.
With every honk, the past takes flight,
Oh, how the concrete spills its night!

Neon lights, they flicker and gleam,
While rats in tuxedos chase a dream.
A traffic jam becomes a dance,
Where lost shoes find their second chance!

The bus driver hums an old refrain,
As he dodges puddles like a game of rain.
Graffiti whispers in colors bold,
Chasing memories that never get old!

Yet amidst the chaos, laughter survives,
As squirrels plot their nutty dives.
Urban tales in the concrete maze,
In the end, they leave us amazed!

Breath of a Forgotten House

Once a palace, now a shamble,
Ghosts in slippers hold a ramble.
Dust bunnies dance with glee,
As the floorboards creak 'What's that, a bee?!'

The curtains weep in a cheeky draught,
While the attic holds the clown's lost craft.
A fridge hums songs of moldy cheer,
Summoning noises only cats can hear!

The lightbulb flickers like responding flair,
'Come play cards!' says a chair with flair.
Toothless grins from forgotten dolls,
Plotting mischief in these silent halls!

In this house where echoes jeer,
Every corner brings a funny cheer.
Memories shaped in laughter loud,
In the stillness, joy is allowed!

Secrets Behind Stalwart Gables

Behind these strong roofs, tales ensue,
Where the builder's squirrels conspire too.
With exposed beams holding stories tight,
Whispering secrets late at night!

The chimney puffs with comical poise,
While raccoons engage in their noisy ploys.
A garden gnome strikes a silly pose,
Hiding laughter, a humorous prose!

The rafters creak and the windows sigh,
As the wind sings songs to the passing sky.
What's that? A catfishing stay-at-home?
In gables' shade, they all can roam!

With each gust, the stories blend,
Inviting laughter that never ends.
In gable's embrace, the spirits play,
Beneath the quirkiness of each day!

Silhouettes of Silent Struggles

In the shadows where mischief thrives,
Silhouettes dance like wiggly hives.
A struggle here, a tussle there,
As if each wall has a tale to share!

Beneath the streetlight's watchful glare,
Two bushes dispute who gets more air.
'Not your turf!' one boldly claims,
While crickets laugh at the silly games!

The pavement cracks with witty lines,
As ants march out with their quirky signs.
'We're on strike!' they seem to say,
For crumbs that fly but never stay!

Yet through it all, the giggles rise,
Whispers of joy, a sweet surprise.
In struggles brightened by humor's light,
The silly show continues its flight!

Silenced Stories Underfoot

In every creak, a tale is found,
Mismatched socks, lost and found.
The floorboards giggle in surprise,
As crumbs confess to kitchen spies.

Old shoes gossip with dusty shoes,
Trading secrets of morning blues.
A hidden dance of rogue old chairs,
While cats plot schemes with devil-may-cares.

Whispers Beneath the Plaster

A secret squeak from plastered walls,
As laughter bounces down the halls.
Tiny mice holding court at night,
Pass whispers wrapped in pure delight.

Where dust bunnies hold their rave,
And cobwebs spin tales that misbehave.
Spry shadows pirouette at ease,
While the wallpaper giggles with the breeze.

Dialogues of the Dusk

Under starry skies, they start to chat,
A lamp post jokes, 'Look at that cat!'
Curtains sway as if in tune,
Pillows whisper to the kindly moon.

Ghostly giggles in the twilight,
As chairs exchange their tales of fright.
Dusk dialogues run long and deep,
With bedtime stories meant for sleep.

Sheltered Echoes of Time

In nooks and crannies, memories hide,
An echo laughs, 'Come take a ride!'
Timid clocks with their tick-tock jokes,
Prank the shadows, and tease the folks.

Beneath the stairs, the echoes play,
With socks that dance the night away.
Old hats making friends with dust,
As stories linger, grow, and rust.

The Language of Cold Concrete

These chilly slabs of glee, so bold,
They gossip in tones both crispy and cold.
A tickle of whispers from gravelly seams,
As they plot their pranks and laugh at our dreams.

In the morning light, they giggle and squeak,
Making jokes about us, oh, how they sneak.
With cracks that conspire, and a playful grin,
Concrete confessions, let the fun begin!

Each step we take, they'll echo with flair,
Reminding us gently, no need for despair.
For under their surface, humor flows free,
Like a comedy show, just for you and me.

When rain drops fall and puddles appear,
Concrete holds secrets, and a bit of cheer.
So next time you walk on their sturdy embrace,
Remember their jokes, and join in the race!

Soft Echoes in Hidden Corridors

In hallways where laughter likes to roam,
Whispers of friends call it their home.
A giggle, a snicker, a faint little shout,
Bouncing off corners that never stay out.

Shadows of joy twist and stretch in the light,
As footsteps create their own silly flight.
Don't mind the echoes, they're just having fun,
Racing through places where secrets outrun.

Tickled by echoes from ages ago,
The corridors chuckle, putting on a show.
With every soft murmur, they sing and they sway,
Playing hide and seek, inviting us to play.

So wander these passages, let laughter find you,
In this sweet labyrinth where giggles break through.
For in the stillness, the jesters do bloom,
With whispers to dance in the soft, silent room.

Tales Imprinted on Faded Facades

Old bricks knock-knock, with stories to tell,
Of quirky mischief and a very tall elf.
Peeling paint shows laughter, the colors still bright,
Each crack a reminder of joy and delight.

Faded facades wear a grin, oh so sly,
With tales of the past that never say die.
Paint us a picture with each charming flake,
Of the pranks that were pulled for happiness' sake.

In the midst of whispers, they twinkle and grin,
Carvings of laughter where memories spin.
Under the sunsets, they clap with such ease,
For every old tale brings a giggle, a tease.

So stroll past the walls, let your heart feel the fun,
Each façade a storyteller, daringly done.
In the light of their history, joy's never far,
With a wink and a whisper, they twinkle like stars.

Ghosts of Laughter Lost in Time

In the corners they linger, with chuckles to share,
Ghosts of old jokes float freely in the air.
They tickle the silence with whispers so bright,
A haunting of humor fills up the night.

Once tangled in shadows, now dance in the light,
These phantoms of laughter, what a curious sight.
They play hide and seek with a wink and a roar,
While ticklish breezes rustle doors once more.

So if you hear giggles where echoes reside,
Know they're lingering softly, inviting your smile.
For every old chuckle that slips through the years,
Is a ghost of good times that washes our fears.

Embrace all the silliness; let your heart climb,
Join the revelry of those lost to time.
For laughter's a spirit that never will fade,
In the realm of the giggles, together we've played.

Heartbeats of the Hollow

In the old tree trunk, a squirrel chats,
Talking to shadows and hiding from cats.
His acorn stash is a mischief galore,
He's naming them all—each a lore.

A breeze sneaks in with a giggle and twist,
It tickles the leaves, too good to resist.
The branches are laughing, they dance in delight,
As critters make plans for a wild, silly night.

The owls drop puns like a feather-light tease,
While rabbits roll over, all weak in the knees.
Whispers abound with cheeky little grins,
As even the moon can't help but join in.

Every nook holds a riddle, a jest,
In this hollow so rich, who needs all the rest?
With echoes of laughter, it's clear as the day,
That here, even silence can't help but play.

The Language of Lattices

A picket fence knows more than it lets on,
With secrets of squirrels and dusk till dawn.
It leans to the side like it's had too much fun,
In the chorus of crickets, it sways just for one.

The windows are winking, oh what a sight,
Their panes are just gossiping all through the night.
They trade little stories, like tips on a prize,
As shadows twist round with a twinkle in their eyes.

A garden of gossip blooms under their guard,
Where cucumbers gossip and zucchinis act hard.
Each flower's a whisper, a giggle in bloom,
As daisies plot dances beneath the bright moon.

With every creak, there's a chuckle to share,
In a lattice of laughter that drifts through the air.
So listen real closely, you might catch the thrill,
In the language of lattices that always stand still.

Beneath the Surface of Stillness

The pond lays flat like a mirror of glee,
Where fish throw a party, just wait and you'll see.
They splash like it's fun, bubbling up from below,
Sending ripples that giggle and twirl to and fro.

Each lily pad's got a dance of its own,
With frogs as the judges, their whispers have grown.
They croak and they hop, what a sight to behold,
In a world of stillness, where laughter is bold.

The dragonflies zip with a wink and a smile,
Racing the clouds for a good little while.
Water bugs play tag, with a flick and a flop,
In the quiet of calm where the fun never stops.

So if you stroll by, hear the chuckles, my friend,
For beneath the still surface, the joy has no end.
With secrets of merriment waiting to be found,
In the dance of the quiet, the silliness abounds.

Veils of Forgotten Tales

In the attic, old boxes stack up with a grin,
Full of hats, shoes, and where in the world have they been?
Dust motes are dancing in the sunlight's warm glow,
While forgotten tales whisper with a giggly flow.

The trunks on the shelf start their chatter at night,
About socks that were lost in a marvelous flight.
There's a coat that held parties, how many? Who knows!
With stories of mishaps as silly as those.

A teddy bear's tale of a brave, daring quest,
To steal all the popcorn and become quite the guest.
With laughter and smiles, they recall every gig,
As they plot one more caper, just a little big.

So peek into corners where dust bunnies sway,
And they'll share the old tales in a funny, sweet way.
For within the veils of what once was alive,
There's a symphony of laughter that still seems to thrive.

The Hidden Narratives of Tattered Facades

Beneath the chipped paint, secrets reside,
A squirrel in a hat, taking odd pride.
With every small scratch, a loud laugh erupts,
As the plump pigeon jests, all well-cupped.

The flowerpots gossip, they giggle and sway,
In the sun's warm embrace, they dream of ballet.
An old tire swings, like a comedian's ring,
Trading tales with the bees on a collective fling.

Chipped bricks can chuckle, don't underestimate,
They whisper the tales of a wild first date.
"Did you hear," they nod, "of the cat in the night?
He wore a tuxedo and danced till daylight!"

Every crack has a story, a jest, or a pun,
Amongst the curls of ivy, the fun has begun.
Tattered edges laugh, as parables spin,
In a world full of echoes, let the humor win.

Fractured Moments in Quiet Abodes

In the shadows, a broom has some fights,
With dust bunnies plotting their escape rights.
Chairs have opinions, though they can't talk,
But listen close, you'll hear them squawk.

Pillows hold giggles from sleepover schemes,
Where fairies debate on the best bedtime dreams.
A lamp flickers gossip of light bulbs in woe,
As cats take their throne in a warm, soft glow.

Walls do their best, while they're out of the loop,
With echoes of laughter, they form a big troupe.
"Who hoarded the snacks?" one corner will shout,
While the ceiling rolls its eyes, "Please, not again, out!"

In quiet abodes, mirth cannot hide,
Even the fridge knows when fun is applied.
So here's to the moments, both jest and repose,
In quirky havens where comedy grows.

Dialogues Lost to Erosion

As wind howls secrets in a cracking facade,
The newspaper's moan is forever a charade.
"Have you heard," the stones gossip with grace,
"Of the dog that could dance? Quite the funny case!"

The fence with splinters mutters with mirth,
Recalling the days of fantastic rebirth.
"I once was a picket, so proud and so tall,
Until a raccoon thought it'd be fun to brawl."

Erosion brings laughs, not just crumbles and dust,
In cracks life continues; in laughter, we trust.
The twigs in the wind weave a comical tune,
As the moon peeks in slyly, grinning like a cartoon.

In dialogues lost, the humor remains,
With each faded story, a chuckle still reigns.
So wander among ruins, be open and free,
To catch the hilarity of history's spree.

The Rhythm of Stone and Silence

In quietude, stones tap a poignant beat,
Echoing laughter right under your seat.
The cobblestones dance in a jig so quaint,
As a hedgehog spins tales no one can paint.

Silence has rhythm, like a drum made of dust,
With echoes of laughter, it's always a must.
Pigeons puff up, wearing suits made of grime,
While the sunlight chuckles, keeping perfect time.

Patched pathways hum tunes of long-gone feet,
"Did you hear about that pickle? He couldn't take the heat!"
Every stone has a jest, a tickle, a tease,
In the still of the day, it's a comedy breeze.

So let's tap our toes to the stories they keep,
In this rhythm of silence, where giggles run deep.
For humor is timeless, like rocks in a row,
A dance of the echoes, come join the show!

Fragmented Realities Embedded in Stone

In a house of bricks, a cat sits tight,
Hearing tales of ghosts at night.
A creaky floor, a muffled sound,
Is that laughter, or a clown unbound?

A crack in the wall, where secrets dwell,
A pickle jar whispering, 'Do tell!'
With every bump and every bump,
The furniture shares a little jump.

The toilet rumbles, as if to say,
'It's me who's the king, in my flush ballet!'
While ceiling fans spin tales I'm sure,
About dust bunnies' dance, a quirky tour.

In every nook, a giggle's born,
As shadows stretch with the early morn.
What fun it is, to have such cheer,
In a home where even walls are queer.

Sentinels of Secrets Embracing Solitude

Behind the mural, a secret plot,
A squirrel in tights, quite the shot!
He steals a snack, a nut or three,
While old paint peels in glee with me.

The clock ticks loudly, a grand old tease,
As mice play tag with the summer breeze.
'Who's ahead?', the shadows ask,
In a game where time's the only task.

A lonely chair spins tales of yore,
Of mismatched socks and a cat's encore.
The air is filled with chuckles faint,
From memories bonded, not of restraint.

Oh whispering corners, how bold you stand,
With secrets molded by a playful hand.
Each sound a riddle, a jest, a cheer,
In solitude's embrace, we're all sincere.

The Soft Cry of Sturdy Corners

In the kitchen, two cups chat away,
'What's brewing, mate? Is it a tea day?'
The fridge hums songs from the past,
As leftovers joke, hoping they last.

A stubborn chair with a wobbly leg,
I've heard it laugh, it's quite the beg.
'If you sit with me, I might just slip,'
It giggles softly, a playful quip.

Every nook a gossip, every hall a song,
'Where's that sock? It shouldn't be long!'
The echoes chuckle, as if they know,
Of mischief made where no one will go.

A window winked with a gust of breeze,
Telling tales of homes and bees.
In corners strong, the whispers play,
Funny moments marked, come what may.

Refrains of Walls that Held Dreams

In dreams of paint and plaster bright,
The walls conduct a concert night.
With echoes bouncing off the frames,
Filling the air with silly games.

A jacket hung, it insists on sway,
As if to dance in a funny way.
The coffee pot burbles rhymes and verse,
A bubbling bard in a caffeinated universe.

And under stairs, a hat lays low,
Whispering secrets from long ago.
A teddy bear chuckles with delight,
At shadows racing past in the light.

In the realm of dreams, laughter's found,
Where each room's magic knows no bound.
Life's awkwardness, a perfect theme,
In a home where every wall can dream.

Remnants of Life in the Gaps

In shadows deep, the dust bunnies roam,
They hide from the light, far away from home.
With giggles and sneezes, they dance like the breeze,
A furry parade of allergies and tease.

Stuck in old corners, their laughter rings clear,
They plot their escape with a pinch of good cheer.
Each speck holds a story, a tiny old tale,
Of coffee spills, crumbs, and the great pizza fail.

Behind every crack, there's a memory bright,
A lonely lost sock plotting its flight.
In the echoes of silence, they caper and skip,
Just don't let the humans get them in a grip!

So raise up a glass to the quirks of the dust,
To whimsies and oddities, it's really a must.
For life's little remnants, we'll chuckle and clap,
And treasure their antics, like one big mishap.

Serenades of Solitude Yet Unheard

In the hush of a room, the spoons start to hum,
A serenade sweet, but it's not from the drum.
The forks join the chorus, clinks in delight,
While the pans sway together, it's quite a sight!

Lonely old chairs have their songs of their own,
They creak and they moan, like they're never alone.
With whispers absurd, they share all their woes,
Of chipped little legs and the scuffs on their toes.

The fridge keeps on singing, a cold, chilly tune,
About leftovers yearning to dance beneath the moon.
With ketchup confessions and mustard so sly,
They giggle behind doors, as they wink with a sigh.

A raucous affair in a home without sound,
Where cutlery choruses and echoes abound.
In solitude wrapped, they find joy in their art,
This orchestra of objects, not one plays a part.

Heartbeats of Echoing Enclosures

In the closet's embrace, the shoes have a chat,
They gossip 'bout journeys and where they all sat.
From flip-flops and boots, to stilettos with flair,
They need no permission to spill all their fare.

The scarves coil and twirl, in colors so bold,
They weave through the moments, both timid and cold.
With secrets enshrined in their soft silken folds,
They laugh at the times when the rain made them mold!

Beneath the old bed, there's a dust-covered toy,
Who dreams of adventures, of pure, goofy joy.
With wobble and jiggle, it's ready to go,
In playful rebellion, leaping, a show!

Each space has a heartbeat, a rhythm unseen,
Where time tick-tocks softly, a sweet little scene.
Together they murmur, their voices a hum,
In enclosures alive, where the laughter is from.

The Quiet Chorus of Longing Walls

In corners unnoticed, the wallpaper sighs,
With patterns that blink and some very short lies.
The paint's peeling laughter, it chuckles in jest,
As it dreams of bright colors and manages best.

The pictures once framed, now with dust are in queues,
They gossip of places, of moments, and views.
With frames all askew, they plot a new role,
To quit being still and embrace some new soul.

Baseboards hold tales of the little ones' feet,
Who raced through the house with the rhythm so sweet.
Now they stand quiet, but don't be misled,
For in dreams they dance on, just like they once tread!

The echoes of whispers in this cozy den,
Play hide and seek 'til we all count to ten.
With a smile on their face, they welcome it all,
Together they sway in the dance of the wall.

Murmurs Beneath the Surface

Between the cracks, a secret giggle,
An echo of laughter, oh so little.
A brick slips, says, 'Why so glum?'
The paint replies, 'I'm just numb!'

I heard a pebble tell a pun,
About a snail out for some fun.
It slipped and slid, oh what a sight,
Giggling, 'I'm just out for a bite.'

A shadow sneezes, 'Bless this place!'
The moss responds, 'In your grace!'
A worm climbs up, with quite the flair,
And says, 'Excuse me, do you share?'

Under layers, stories dwell,
Each crease and crack, a jolly spell.
Who knew that bricks could hold such cheer,
In every whisper, joy is near!

Boundaries of Forgotten Stories

A door creaks open, then it sighs,
'Care for a joke?' it slyly implies.
The hinges chuckle, join the delight,
Their laughter echoing into the night.

Ghosts of laughter hang in the air,
What did the lamp say? 'I'm quite rare!'
A chair winks, 'I used to dance,
Now I just sit and watch romance.'

A window grins, a clever cazoo,
Sings of lovers that once said 'I do.'
Their whispers twirl like leaves in fall,
Dancing their way past the garden wall.

Stories forgotten, yet still, they play,
In shadows where memories sway.
With every creak, a tale takes flight,
Creating joy from sheer delight!

Veils of Stone and Memory

In city streets, the stones confer,
'Did you hear that? A gentle purr!'
The gravel laughs, 'That's just a cat,
It dreams of pouncing, how about that?'

A lamppost sways, 'What a sight!
I've held the sun, but love the night!'
The cobblestones can't help but chime,
'Best stories lurk, outside of time!'

A breeze giggles, 'I'm but a tease,
Tickling leaves, making them freeze!'
The fountain splashes, 'Join my spree,
Laughter's the best, don't you agree?'

Though carved from stone, they're full of glee,
Each whisper a playful decree.
In laughter's embrace, they find their way,
Through veils of memory, night and day!

Hushed Conversations at Dusk

As night descends with a goofy grin,
The sky speaks softly, 'Let's begin!'
The stars spill secrets, bursting bright,
'Ever been caught in a moth's flight?'

Beneath the trees, the shadows play,
'A leaf just slipped, where'd it sway?'
A whispering root says, 'A wild ride,
Let's leave behind the blushing tide.'

The breeze passes by, with a wink and nod,
'Take a chance, don't be a clod!'
Laughter ripples through branches low,
Jokes exchanged, it's quite the show.

In this hush, where giggles thrive,
A language of joy keeps dreams alive.
As dusk wraps around like a cuddly shawl,
Every whisper here, is a fun-loving call!

Residue of Dreams on Stony Surfaces

In the alley where pigeons do roam,
There's a mural that just can't find home.
A cat winks at me, with a grin so wide,
As if it's the one who's taken a ride.

Graffiti smiles, they shout and they sing,
Forget all the heaviness life tends to bring.
A squirrel in a hat plays the jazz on the side,
While the bricks blush azure with laughter and pride.

The echoes of giggles bounce off the stone,
As cranky old neighbors complain and moan.
Lost on the pavement, a bubblegum dream,
Rolls with a twist in a swirl of cream.

A raccoon on a rooftop stars in a show,
With a pie in his paws, he steals the old glow.
Can't take life too serious, that's what they say,
When surfaces chatter, and colors play.

Ethereal Whispers from Weathered Heights

Up on the ledge where clouds like to frolic,
A statue's been caught in a whisper so squalid.
It rolls its stone eyes like an old, wise chap,
Saying, "Hey! Snatch that fruitcake, just take a nap!"

Chimneys gossip, exchanging old tales,
About cats with no leashes and mischief in trails.
The wind tugs at hats that dance with delight,
While a grumpy old crow guards the fallacy's flight.

Moss dances too, with a wiggle and cheer,
"Come join in, dear buddy! There's room for a beer!"
The rooftops chuckle at clouds roaming free,
In this circus of whispers, you're never lonely.

Leaves on the ground know all the faux pas,
They chuckle and crinkle, revealing their scars.
What's life if not laughter wrapped in a jest?
Where echoes from high just know how to fest!

Shadows Swathed in Brick and Mortar

Beneath a brick arch, shadows collide,
With a wink and a giggle, they try to hide.
A dog on the corner, a laugh in his bark,
Claims the whole place just came out to park.

The sidewalk's a canvas where stories reside,
Old ladies in fedoras engage in a slide.
"Did you see the fly that danced through the air?
It rumored of cupcakes and debonair flair!"

A skateboard rolls by and the bricks cheer loud,
While a pizza slice spins, oh, isn't he proud!
Windows that chatter know all the best quips,
Cracking wise jokes and playful backflips.

In every small crevice, a giggle or two,
Comes from the pavement, from pretense so new.
With shadows that stretch sticky like taffy,
They tell of pure silliness, oh how they're happy!

The Unraveling of Old Conversations

Two old benches chat with a squeaky old tune,
About squirrels who throw nuts under the moon.
"He swiped my sandwich, I swear he was sly!"
The other bench chuckles, "You'll see him fly!"

Worn-out lampposts, they gossip and sway,
About pigeons who strut on their elegant way.
"There goes Miss Plumage, who thinks she's so grand,
With a flair for the fabulous, isn't life planned?"

The pavement rolls out a welcoming mat,
For mischief, for laughter, and me and my hat.
"Did you hear what the curb said to the street?
'Get in line, old chap, it's time for a meet!'"

Echoes of chuckles escape from the cracks,
A symphony of stories, with no need for tracks.
Thus, underneath light, they brew delight,
In these old conversations, the world feels just right.

Hushed Conversations in the Gaps

In a house built of silence, they speak,
A fridge hums secrets, so unique.
The cat drops a plate, oh what a show,
And the sofa just giggles, don't you know?

The clock ticks a joke, time's in on it,
Creaky stairs whisper, they just can't quit.
A ghost in the attic trying a rhyme,
While shadows debate about the next mime.

The curtains are eavesdroppers, it's bizarre,
Fluttering round like they just hit the bar.
With every pet sneeze, laughter ignites,
Even the dust bunnies join in the fights.

So raise a glass to the nonsense contained,
In echoes of laughter, well-maintained.
A home filled with chatter that's seldom clear,
In the gaps where we mumble, we hold it dear.

Soundscapes of Solitude

In the stillness, the kettle steams,
Whispering tales of unshared dreams.
The toaster pops out a slice of bread,
As if making jokes about what's said.

The slippers shuffle, in no hurry at all,
While a couch potato plans the next brawl.
Dust motes dancing in lazy delight,
As the ceiling fan stirs up more than light.

A teaspoon sings to the sugar bowl,
As if discussing the day's new role.
The echo of laughter from yesterday's feast,
Makes the quiet moments feel like a beast.

So here's to the soundscape, gentle and rare,
Where humor bubbles, floating in the air.
Every creak and sigh knows how to play,
In a symphony of silence, night and day.

The Poetry Held Within

In the corners, where echoes reside,
The poetry waits, oh, what a ride.
A mouse in the pantry scribbles a verse,
While the broom sweeps dreams, free of the curse.

Chairs have opinions, though they're not loud,
They gossip about the guest, quite proud.
The plants in the window nod to the beat,
As if to say, 'Life's bittersweet.'

A sock on the floor shares a tale of woe,
Says the dryer's a beast, steals all the show.
The TV's been plotting a drama for months,
While the fridge tells jokes, layering the hunts.

So gather 'round for the stories untold,
In the poetry once wrapped in silence so bold.
Laughter hides deep in the hummed refrain,
In the rhythm of echoes that drive us insane.

Reflections in the Quiet

In the stillness, reflections come alive,
A mirror grins back, sharp as a hive.
The floorboards creak with a shy little laugh,
Spying on thoughts like a curious calf.

A lamp with its shade flirts with the wall,
While the wallpaper blushes, feeling small.
The window decorates dreams with the sun,
Making light of whispers, oh isn't it fun?

The rug has seen dances, both silly and grand,
Some moves so odd, they can't understand.
In the shadows, a chuckle escapes from the hall,
As a name tag drops, not meant at all.

So let the quiet be the stage for the jest,
Where whispers collide and laughter's the guest.
In the oddest of corners, may joy find you here,
In the reflections that shimmer, so crystal clear.

Ethereal Melodies in the Brickwork

In brick-lined trails, a tune does play,
The mortar hums, come out to sway.
A dance of ghosts with socks askew,
They stomp and twirl, much like we do.

The uncle's voice, a croaky song,
He says he's right but he's all wrong.
That chandelier, it swings a bit,
A phantom's laugh? No, just my wit.

When shadows joke and shadows jest,
I swear they put my sanity to test.
At midnight feasts, they munch on cheese,
With toast and jam, if you please!

So, let's not fret for time misplaced,
In such odd company, we're all faced.
The bricks may shine, the laughter rise,
In spirits' tune, the noise defies.

The Unseen Dialogue of Lost Souls

Two specters sit on a wooden chair,
Arguing who has the better hair.
With caps and curls, their fashion's bold,
Yet, where to find a stylist? Cold!

They gossip 'bout the ghosts of yore,
While floating drinks just spill on the floor.
A phantom says, 'Did you hear the news?'
Last week's scare? Too much to lose!

As they clash o'er spectral wine,
Old sage claims he once was divine.
But who believed the tales he spun,
Of chasing cats just for the fun?

So, in the dark, they share their wits,
With punchlines made from little bits.
For unseen souls, their humor's grand,
Sprinkling laughs across this land.

Rooms Echoing with Past Lives

In faded rooms, a laugh persists,
Where chairs still dance and doors still twist.
A family of echoes, quite the crew,
Dressed in sheets, they bid adieu.

The grandpa ghost steals my last fry,
I cry, 'Hey there, that's not your pie!'
He winks and spills his coffee cup,
I bet he thinks he's in a sup-up.

The wallpaper sighs, it can't be tamed,\nA history there, yet none are blamed.
They throw a party while I just snooze,
Who knew the past could play the blues?

But while I'm lost in dream's embrace,
Those past lives sing with flair and grace.
In echoes loud, the room does thrive,
With silly laughs, they feel alive!

Resonance of Unexplored Spaces

In corners dark, two mice debate,
A cheese platter set, but why so late?
The shortages of crumbs and cheese,
They plot in whispers on their knees.

An old cat listens, thinks it's sly,
While dreaming of a tasty pie.
But then it sneezes, scares them both,
The mice bolt quick; oh, what a troth!

Spaces left by humans' haste,
Now filled with mischief, none to waste.
They swing from shelves, dodging dust,
Creating chaos! It's a must.

So while we dwell in explored terrain,
Remember the laughter and the pain.
In every nook, a tale's awake,
In empty places, let joy partake.

www.ingramcontent.com/pod-product-compliance
Lightning Source LLC
Chambersburg PA
CBHW070335120526
44590CB00017B/2899